COMMUNITY ENGAGEMENT PROJECT

CEP (DISCIPLINE SPECIFIC CORE COURSE)

DR. SHAIKH TAUFIQ KHALIL
DR. RAMESH BODHANKAR
MS.KAVTIA J. JUIKAR
MRS TEJAL BHAVE
MRS ASHWINI Y. DESAI

Made with ♥ on the Notion Press Platform
www.notionpress.com

To my beloved family—my parents, whose guidance and encouragement have been my foundation; my wife, Sabenoor, for her unwavering support and understanding; and to my friends who have shared this journey with me.

With heartfelt gratitude to Dr. M.S. Khurade, our Dean, and Dr. Sucharita Sarkar, our Principal, for their invaluable mentorship and belief in this endeavor. A special acknowledgment to Dr. Salim Ansari, whose insights and support have been a source of strength throughout.

Thank you all for inspiring me to pursue this work and for being by my side every step of the way.

Contents

Foreword

India's socioeconomic landscape has experienced profound changes over the past few decades, resulting in varied forms of livelihood across urban and rural spaces. To build a comprehensive understanding of these transformations, one must explore the essence of rural and urban livelihoods, the role of local government institutions, and the impact of national development programs.

This book, *Community Engagement Project*, offers a structured guide for commerce students seeking to develop a grounded knowledge of community dynamics and economic interdependencies. With its focus on hands-on field experience and the role of classroom knowledge in real-world contexts, the book stands as an essential resource. Students will not only gain insights into development programs like the Pradhan Mantri Awaas Yojana and MGNREGA but also understand the mechanisms of local self-governance and the contribution of Self-Help Groups to socioeconomic empowerment.

For students, faculty, and professionals interested in fostering positive societal impacts through informed engagement, this text serves as a foundational resource. It equips readers with the knowledge needed to navigate, analyze, and contribute meaningfully to community and economic development. It is with pleasure and respect that I introduce this work, knowing it will inspire students to engage thoughtfully with the communities around them.

Preface

The purpose of writing *Community Engagement Project* is to bridge the gap between theoretical learning and the practical realities of community engagement in India. Through structured course content and a focus on hands-on learning, this book empowers students to understand and impact the livelihood challenges and opportunities within both rural and urban communities.

During the development of this text, extensive research was conducted on local institutions, national development programs, and their impact on the everyday lives of Indian citizens. This book is tailored for commerce students who wish to understand socioeconomic structures while gaining insights into local government institutions, employment programs, and development initiatives. The inclusion of numerous case studies, program descriptions, and community stories aims to connect academic knowledge to real-world outcomes.

We hope this book equips students with the tools they need to critically analyze community issues, develop problem-solving skills, and encourage active citizenship.

Acknowledgements

Creating a resource of this scope required the guidance and support of many individuals and organizations. I would like to extend my deepest gratitude to everyone who contributed to this project.

I am particularly thankful to the local government officials, community leaders, and Self-Help Group representatives who shared their insights and experiences, providing real-world perspectives essential to this text. My heartfelt thanks go to the faculty and colleagues at DTSS College of Commerce, whose encouragement and expertise were invaluable during the writing process.

Special acknowledgment goes to my family, whose constant support made this project possible, and to my students, whose enthusiasm for community engagement inspired every chapter. Finally, I am grateful to the Government of India and the Indian Statistical Department for their comprehensive data and program details, which have enriched the factual foundation of this book.

Prologue

India's development landscape is a complex tapestry of diverse communities, local institutions, and evolving policies aimed at uplifting rural and urban livelihoods. This book delves into the heartbeat of these initiatives, exploring the sources of income that sustain both rural and urban societies, the local government bodies that shape communities, and the national programs transforming lives.

Through on-ground stories, case studies, and analytical insights, we explore the strengths and challenges of these programs, aiming to present a holistic view of India's developmental journey. This work is a tribute to the resilience of communities and the enduring efforts of those committed to a more inclusive future.

Introduction

Understanding community dynamics is crucial to developing effective and sustainable development strategies. In India, local communities serve as the backbone of economic and social progress, especially in rural areas where traditional livelihoods persist despite modernization. Urban areas, too, present unique challenges, balancing modern industry with the needs of a diverse population.

This book, *Community Engagement Project*, is designed as an academic resource for students of commerce who wish to expand their knowledge of the multifaceted Indian economy. Through modules that cover rural and urban livelihoods, local governance structures, and national programs, the course provides students with a well-rounded perspective on how government initiatives and community-based efforts shape the socioeconomic landscape.

The book is divided into two modules. The first explores local economic practices and the institutions that support them. The second module delves into national development initiatives that address everything from healthcare and housing to education and employment. This text aims not only to provide knowledge but to inspire students to apply their classroom learning in a manner that benefits society, reinforcing the idea that meaningful change begins at the grassroots level.

By completing this course, students will develop a keen understanding of local governance, economic practices, and the importance of active community engagement, all while working towards positive societal change.

Syllabus

Module	Chapters	Number of Lectures
Module I	**Chapter 1: Understanding Local Economy and Livelihood** - Agriculture and Agrarian Livelihoods - Non-Farm Livelihoods and Artisans - Entrepreneurship in Rural/Urban Markets - Migrant Labour Dynamics	5
	Chapter 2: Local Institutions - Local Self-Government and Panchayati Raj - Self-Help Groups (SHGs) - Local Administrative Bodies	5
Module II	**Chapter 3: National Development Programs** - Overview of Key Programs: *Sarva Shiksha Abhiyan, Beti Bachao Beti Padhao, Ayushman Bharat, Swachh Bharat, PM Awaas Yojana* - Vocational and Skill Development: *Skill India, Gram Panchayat Decentralised Planning* - Employment and Welfare Schemes: *NRLM, MGNREGA, SHRAM Portal* - Infrastructure and Sustainability: *Jal Jeevan Mission, SFURTI, Atma Nirbhar Bharat*	10
Total		**20**

Enter Caption

Contents

CHAPTER ONE

Understanding Local Economy and Livelihood

Objective:

This section introduces the concept of local economies and various livelihoods that sustain rural and urban communities.

1.1 Introduction to Local Economy and Livelihood

In any society, livelihood is the way people earn a living to support themselves and their families. The local economy is shaped by diverse activities, from agriculture to artisanal crafts, and from small-scale entrepreneurship to service industries. This economic diversity not only sustains the population but also contributes to regional growth and resilience. Understanding these components is essential to grasp the socio-economic dynamics that define both rural and urban areas.

1.2 Agriculture and Agrarian Livelihoods

Agriculture has traditionally formed the backbone of rural economies in India, engaging around 58% of the rural population as per the National Sample Survey Organization (NSSO) and playing a crucial role in food security, economic stability, and employment. While the sector has evolved, it remains central to rural livelihoods and sustenance.

Types of Agricultural Practices

1. Subsistence Farming

- **Definition and Scope**: Subsistence farming is characterized by small-scale operations aimed at providing for the household's food needs, often without significant surplus for sale. This type of farming dominates in regions with small landholdings, limited resources, and minimal access to advanced technologies.

- **Current Data**: According to the *Agriculture Census 2015-16*, around 86% of Indian farmers own less than 2 hectares of land, making them small or marginal farmers, primarily engaged in subsistence farming. In the absence of irrigation facilities, most depend on seasonal rains, limiting the number of crops they can grow annually.
- **Impact**: Subsistence farming is highly vulnerable to climate change, and farmers often lack financial security, with an estimated 25.7% of rural households living below the poverty line (as per the *National Family Health Survey*).

2. Commercial Farming

- **Definition and Scope**: Commercial farming focuses on producing crops and livestock on a large scale for sale in local and international markets, aiming to maximize yield and profit. This approach often involves the cultivation of cash crops like sugarcane, cotton, wheat, rice, and spices.
- **Current Data**: India ranks among the top global producers of crops like rice (second largest), wheat (second largest), and cotton. According to the *Department of Agriculture, Cooperation & Farmers Welfare*, the 2022-23 estimated production of rice was around 130 million tonnes, with wheat at approximately 112 million tonnes.
- **Impact**: Commercial farming contributes significantly to the Indian economy. However, large-scale farming requires higher input costs for seeds, fertilizers, and pesticides. While mechanization is more prevalent in this sector, small farmers often face high initial costs, limiting participation.

Agricultural Productivity

Agricultural productivity in India has seen steady improvement, yet it remains below global averages. Productivity is affected by a combination of environmental, technological, and socio-economic factors.

1. **Soil Quality**: Soil health is foundational to productivity, but challenges like nutrient depletion and soil erosion are common. The *Indian Council of Agricultural Research (ICAR)* reports that approximately 120 million hectares of land suffer from soil degradation, impacting yield.
2. **Water Availability**: India's agriculture is highly dependent on monsoons, with nearly 60% of cropped area lacking reliable irrigation.

Data from the *Ministry of Water Resources* shows that only about 45% of the gross cropped area is irrigated, with groundwater levels dropping annually due to over-extraction.

3. **Weather Patterns**: Changing weather patterns have led to erratic rainfall, droughts, and floods. Data from the *Indian Meteorological Department (IMD)* for 2023 highlights an increase in extreme weather events, impacting crop cycles and yields.
4. **Access to Technology**: The government has launched several programs to modernize agriculture, including the Pradhan Mantri Fasal Bima Yojana (crop insurance) and Kisan Credit Cards. However, small and marginal farmers often have limited access to these technologies. The *Agricultural Census 2015-16* reports that mechanization and technology penetration are more concentrated in larger farms.
5. **Sustainable Practices**: Organic farming is gaining traction as an eco-friendly alternative. According to the *Ministry of Agriculture & Farmers' Welfare*, organic farming coverage increased from 0.3 million hectares in 2014 to over 2.78 million hectares in 2023, with India exporting organic products worth $1.04 billion in 2022.

Challenges Facing Agriculture

Despite these advancements, agriculture in India faces significant challenges that threaten its sustainability and productivity.

1. Climate Change

- **Impact of Climate Change**: Climate change affects agriculture through unpredictable rainfall, heatwaves, and shifting seasons. Studies from the *Indian Council of Agricultural Research (ICAR)* indicate that by 2050, climate change could reduce the yields of key crops like wheat and rice by 10-15%.
- **Real-World Data**: In 2022, extreme weather affected nearly 3.6 million hectares of cropland, according to the *Ministry of Agriculture*. The IMD reported over 200 heatwaves across northern India in the summer of 2023, leading to crop losses, particularly in wheat and mustard.

2. Resource Scarcity

- **Water**: Limited access to water and depleting groundwater levels have become a critical challenge, particularly in states like Punjab, Haryana, and Tamil Nadu. According to *NITI Aayog's* 2019 Composite Water Management Index, 21 Indian cities, including Delhi and Bengaluru, could run out of groundwater in the near future, threatening agricultural sustainability.
- **Seeds and Fertilizers**: The availability and cost of quality seeds and fertilizers remain issues for many farmers. Government subsidies have attempted to alleviate the cost burden; however, many farmers still report financial strain due to rising fertilizer costs. *Agriculture Ministry* data shows a 16% rise in fertilizer costs between 2020 and 2022, affecting smallholders most acutely.

3. Market Access

- **Supply Chain Gaps**: Farmers often face challenges in accessing markets, resulting in income instability. Small and marginal farmers lack the resources to transport their goods to large markets and rely on local intermediaries, often accepting lower prices.
- **Government Initiatives**: Programs like eNAM (National Agriculture Market) aim to digitize markets, allowing farmers to sell directly to buyers, bypassing intermediaries. However, adoption rates are low, especially in regions with limited digital infrastructure.
- **Current Data**: A 2022 survey by the *NABARD (National Bank for Agriculture and Rural Development)* found that only 12% of small farmers used eNAM to sell produce, with the majority still dependent on traditional mandis. In the *Agricultural Marketing and Farmer Friendly Reforms Index 2023*, only 10 states scored above 50%, indicating substantial room for improvement in market accessibility.

In summary Agriculture in India faces a complex array of challenges but continues to be central to

rural livelihoods. With approximately 17-18% of GDP derived from agriculture, efforts to modernize,

dapt to climate change, and improve resource access are vital. Government policies and technology initiatives are crucial in addressing these issues, though effective implementation remains a challenge

in achieving sustainability and resilience in Indian agriculture.

1.3 Non-Farm Livelihoods and Artisans

While agriculture remains a central livelihood in rural areas, non-farm activities play an increasingly crucial role in providing alternative income sources. These occupations include artisanal and handicraft work, small-scale manufacturing, and services, all of which contribute significantly to the local economy. According to the *National Sample Survey (NSS)*, around 38% of rural households in India are engaged in non-farm activities, highlighting the importance of diversifying rural income sources.

Artisan and Handicraft Industries

1. Traditional Crafts and Artisanal Work

- **Scope of Artisanal Work:** Traditional crafts such as pottery, weaving, woodwork, metalwork, and handloom textiles are deeply rooted in rural India. These crafts are often family-run, with skills passed down across generations. India is one of the world's largest producers and exporters of handicrafts, and the sector is a key source of employment, especially for women and marginalized communities.
- **Current Data:** According to the *Handicrafts Export Promotion Council*, the handicrafts sector employs over 7 million artisans across the country, contributing around ₹28,000 crores in export revenue annually. The *2021-22 Economic Survey* reported that the handicrafts and handloom sectors collectively contribute around 15% to the country's manufacturing GDP.

2. Challenges in Artisan and Handicraft Industries

Artisans face multiple challenges that hinder growth and sustainability:

- **Lack of Modern Tools and Technology:** Many artisans continue to rely on traditional methods that are labour-intensive and time-consuming. Limited access to modern tools and technology affects their productivity and ability to compete with machine-made goods.
- **Market Reach and Competition:** Artisans often struggle to access larger markets, limiting their sales and income. Competing with factory-made, mass-produced goods, especially from global markets, is challenging. The influx of cheaper products diminishes the demand for handmade crafts.
- **Government Initiatives:** Recognizing these challenges, the government has implemented initiatives like the *Scheme of Fund for Regeneration*

of Traditional Industries (SFURTI). Launched by the Ministry of Micro, Small and Medium Enterprises (MSME), SFURTI aims to modernize traditional industries by providing training, technology upgrades, and market access. Under SFURTI, around 65,000 artisans have benefited from upgraded infrastructure, better equipment, and enhanced design capabilities, as per the Ministry's 2023 report.

- **Real-World Data:** In 2023, the government announced a ₹250 crore budget allocation under SFURTI to support clusters of artisans and craftspeople. Additionally, *One District One Product (ODOP)* aims to create a unique identity for local products, boosting marketing opportunities for artisans in both domestic and global markets.

Services and Small Businesses

The service sector in rural and urban India is a major contributor to non-farm livelihoods, offering an array of opportunities in areas like retail, transportation, repair work, and small-scale trading. These occupations play a critical role in meeting the daily needs of communities and sustaining economic flow.

1. Types of Services in Rural and Urban Economies

- **Retail Shops:** Small retail shops are a staple in both rural and urban communities, providing access to essential goods. According to the *National Statistical Office (NSO)*, rural areas have seen a 15% growth in retail establishments over the past decade, indicating the sector's expansion.
- **Transportation Services:** In rural areas, transportation services range from auto-rickshaws to larger commercial vehicles transporting agricultural produce. Data from the *Ministry of Rural Development* indicates that transportation is a growing sector in rural areas, with 25% of rural non-farm jobs linked to logistics and transportation.
- **Repair and Maintenance Work:** Small repair services, including mechanics, electricians, and appliance repairers, are essential in both rural and urban areas. The NSO estimates that around 1.2 million people are employed in rural repair services, providing stable income for families.

2. Economic Contribution and Challenges

- **Economic Impact**: Services and small businesses not only provide employment but also enhance the circulation of money within the local economy. The *National Rural Employment Guarantee Act (MGNREGA)* has supported this sector by offering infrastructure improvements like road construction, which facilitates easier transportation of goods and services.
- **Challenges Faced by Service Providers**:
  - **Limited Capital**: Many rural entrepreneurs lack access to loans or investment, which restricts their ability to expand or upgrade services.
  - **Market Linkages**: Limited access to markets means that small businesses struggle to scale up or diversify their services.
  - **Infrastructure Gaps**: Rural areas often have limited infrastructure, such as inadequate roads or power supply, impacting service reliability.

3. Government Support and Recent Data

To support the rural service economy, several initiatives have been launched:

- **Deendayal Antyodaya Yojana - National Rural Livelihoods Mission (DAY-NRLM)**: This scheme, implemented by the Ministry of Rural Development, aims to enhance rural livelihoods by encouraging entrepreneurship and small business development. As of 2023, NRLM has assisted over 8 million households in establishing income-generating activities, including small businesses and services.
- **Stand-Up India and MUDRA Loans**: To support small entrepreneurs, particularly women and marginalized groups, the government launched the *Stand-Up India* scheme and *Micro Units Development and Refinance Agency (MUDRA) Loans*. As per the 2023 annual report of MUDRA, ₹ 3.37 lakh crore in loans were sanctioned, benefiting around 7 million small business owners, of whom 60% were from rural areas.

In summary Non-farm livelihoods in India, encompassing artisan industries and small-scale services, are

integralto rural and urban economies. Despite challenges such as limited market reach, technology access, and competition from mass production, these sectors have shown resilience.

With ongoing government initiatives like SFURTI, NRLM, and MUDRA, artisans and small

business owners are receiving increasing support to modernize and expand their operations,

contributing to local economic growth and providing stable incomes for millions of families.

1.4 Entrepreneurship in Rural and Urban Markets

Entrepreneurship is a key driver of economic growth in both rural and urban areas of India, enabling individuals to create businesses, generate employment, and address local needs. With government initiatives supporting skill development, funding access, and infrastructure improvement, entrepreneurship has become more accessible. This section explores the nuances of rural and urban entrepreneurship and the distinct opportunities and challenges each face, backed by real-time data from the Government of India and the Indian Statistical Department.

Rural Entrepreneurship

Rural entrepreneurship is often centered around agriculture and allied sectors, with businesses focusing on food processing, livestock management, agro-based industries, and small-scale manufacturing. These ventures not only create jobs but also help local communities retain their youth by providing viable livelihood options within the village setting.

1. **Agriculture-Related Businesses**

Food Processing and Agro-Based Industries: Rural entrepreneurship frequently involves agro-based industries that add value to agricultural produce. According to the *Ministry of Food Processing Industries*, the food processing sector in India is growing at an annual rate of 11%, creating numerous opportunities in rural areas for setting up processing units for dairy, grains, fruits, and vegetables. For instance, fruit pulp processing units and dairy plants are common ventures in rural areas, especially in states like Maharashtra, Gujarat, and Uttar Pradesh.

Data Insight: As per the *Annual Report of the Ministry of Food Processing Industries (2023)*, the Pradhan Mantri Kisan Sampada Yojana (PMKSY) has helped establish 500 new food processing units in rural India, creating over 1.2 million job opportunities and benefiting approximately 10 million farmers.

1. **Skill Development Initiatives**

The government has implemented various programs to upskill rural entrepreneurs, including the *Skill India Mission*, *Deen Dayal Upadhyaya Grameen Kaushalya Yojana (DDU-GKY)*, and *Rural Self Employment Training Institutes (RSETI)*. These programs provide training in areas like farm management, dairy management, food processing, and digital literacy.

Real-World Impact: Since its launch, Skill India has trained over 10 million rural youth, equipping them with skills for small-scale entrepreneurial activities, as reported by the *Ministry of Skill Development and Entrepreneurship* in 2023. Under RSETI, over 3.5 million people were trained, of whom nearly 70% started small businesses in rural regions.

1. **Challenges Facing Rural Entrepreneurs**

Limited Access to Capital: Access to financial services and loans remains a hurdle for rural entrepreneurs. While the government's *MUDRA Yojana* aims to bridge this gap by offering collateral-free loans, challenges persist in the availability of larger-scale funding for expansion.

Market Access and Infrastructure: Limited access to larger markets, infrastructure gaps (e.g., poor road connectivity), and inadequate storage facilities are key issues. Rural entrepreneurs often rely on local markets, which limits their business reach.

1. **Government Support Programs**

Stand-Up India and MUDRA Yojana: To support entrepreneurship, particularly among marginalized communities, *Stand-Up India* and *MUDRA Yojana* offer financial support. In 2023, over ₹3.5 lakh crore was disbursed to micro-entrepreneurs, 60% of whom were in rural areas.

Urban Entrepreneurship

Urban entrepreneurship is diverse, spanning industries such as retail, technology, creative arts, and manufacturing. Urban entrepreneurs benefit from relatively better infrastructure, access to financial institutions, and proximity to larger markets. This environment fosters innovation, accelerates business growth, and contributes significantly to job creation.

1. **Diverse Industry Opportunities**

Tech Startups: Urban areas, especially metro cities, are home to India's thriving startup ecosystem. According to *NASSCOM*, India ranks third globally in terms of the number of startups, with around 50,000 startups as of 2023. Cities like Bangalore, Delhi NCR, and Mumbai have become hubs for technology-driven ventures in e-commerce, fintech, ed-tech, and health-tech.

Retail and Service Sectors: Urban areas also see a high concentration of retail businesses, food and beverage outlets, and service-oriented businesses, such as beauty, healthcare, and hospitality. The *Ministry of Commerce and Industry* reports that retail is the largest employer in urban regions, accounting for around 15% of urban employment in India.

1. **Access to Finance and Infrastructure**

Funding and Venture Capital: Urban entrepreneurs have better access to venture capital, angel investors, and banks. The *Department for Promotion of Industry and Internal Trade (DPIIT)* noted that urban startups attracted $35 billion in funding in 2022, with a focus on sectors like digital services, renewable energy, and logistics.

Incubators and Accelerators: Urban centers offer robust support systems, such as business incubators and accelerators, which assist startups with mentorship, networking, and financial resources. The *Atal Innovation Mission* under the *NITI Aayog* has established around 150 Atal Incubation Centers (AICs) nationwide, primarily in urban locations, providing support to over 5,000 startups.

3. **Challenges in Urban Entrepreneurship**

Market Saturation: In metropolitan areas, intense competition among startups can make market entry and growth challenging, particularly for new entrants. Established brands and high customer expectations also add to the difficulties.

Cost of Operations: Urban entrepreneurs face high operating costs due to rent, labour, and transportation expenses. According to *The Economic Survey of India (2022)*, operational costs for urban businesses can be up to 40% higher than in rural areas.

4. **Supportive Government Policies**

Startup India Initiative: Launched in 2016, the *Startup India* initiative promotes entrepreneurship by offering tax benefits, simplifying regulations, and enhancing access to funding. By 2023, more than 80,000 startups were recognized under the scheme, receiving benefits that have collectively saved approximately ₹20,000 crores in tax.

Ease of Doing Business Reforms: Initiatives like the *Goods and Services Tax (GST)* and digital platforms for regulatory filings have simplified business operations for urban entrepreneurs, as per the *2023 DPIIT Report*. These measures have helped India improve its global ranking in ease of doing business, encouraging more individuals to venture into entrepreneurship.

In summary Entrepreneurship in both rural and urban areas serves as a powerful economic engine, contributing to job creation, skill development, and community growth. Rural entrepreneurs are instrumental in the agricultural and artisanal sectors, while urban entrepreneurs lead in retail, technology, and service-oriented industries. With targeted government initiatives, skill-building programs, and financial support, India's entrepreneurial ecosystem is continuously evolving, creating opportunities for innovation across diverse landscapes. However, distinct challenges such as infrastructure gaps in rural areas and high operational costs in urban areas highlight the need for tailored policies to further support these ventures.

1.5 Migrant Labour Dynamics

Migrant labour is a cornerstone of India's urban economy and plays a dual role in shaping both rural and urban livelihoods. While migration is often seen as a pathway to better opportunities for individuals, it has significant implications for local economies at both ends of the migration route. The following sections explore the push and pull factors driving migration, as well as its economic and social impacts on rural and urban areas, supported by recent data from the Government of India and Indian statistical sources.

Push and Pull Factors in Migration

Migration in India is driven by a combination of "push" factors from rural areas and "pull" factors from urban centers:

1. **Push Factors:**

- **Limited Employment Opportunities**: The lack of job availability in rural areas, often coupled with low wages, forces people to look elsewhere for income. According to the *National Sample Survey Office (NSSO)*, rural unemployment reached approximately 5.7% in 2023, a factor driving migration to cities with greater job prospects.
- **Agricultural Challenges**: Rural residents often face challenges like unpredictable monsoons, shrinking landholdings, and low productivity, which make agricultural income insufficient. As per the *Agricultural Census 2020-21*, around 85% of farmers in India are small and marginal landholders, making it difficult for them to sustain themselves on agriculture alone.

2. **Pull Factors:**

- **Higher Wages in Urban Centers**: Cities offer relatively higher wages, especially in industries like construction, manufacturing, and services. The *Ministry of Labour and Employment* reported that average daily wages for unskilled labourers are around ₹400–₹500 in urban areas, compared to ₹150–₹200 in rural areas.
- **Better Access to Services and Infrastructure**: Urban areas provide better healthcare, education, and public services. This accessibility motivates rural populations to relocate in hopes of improving their quality of life.

Impact on Local Economies

Migration has distinct economic and social impacts on both rural and urban areas.

1. **In Rural Areas:**

- **Labour Shortages in Agriculture**: Migration often reduces the available workforce for agricultural activities. According to a report by *NITI Aayog*, seasonal migration can lead to a 15%–20% drop in rural labour availability during peak farming seasons. This shortage affects crop production, leading some farmers to shift to less labour-intensive crops or hire external labour, increasing operational costs.
- **Remittances and Economic Support**: Migrants typically send remittances back to their families, providing a crucial income stream

that supports household consumption and investment in rural areas. *Reserve Bank of India* data indicates that remittances contribute up to 30% of the income for households of migrant labourers in certain rural regions. These remittances support local businesses, contribute to home construction, and fund children's education.

2. **In Urban Areas:**

    - **Contribution to Key Industries**: Migrant labour is essential to urban industries like construction, manufacturing, and domestic services. According to the *Ministry of Housing and Urban Affairs*, migrants account for nearly 60% of the labour force in the construction sector. Their role is especially critical in infrastructure projects, which form the backbone of urban expansion and industrial growth.
    - **Strain on Urban Resources**: The influx of migrants can strain urban resources, including housing, sanitation, healthcare, and public transportation. Cities often struggle to accommodate large migrant populations, resulting in the proliferation of informal settlements and slums. According to a *2019 study by the National Institute of Urban Affairs*, more than 40% of migrants live in informal housing due to limited affordable options in cities like Mumbai, Delhi, and Bangalore.
    - **Socioeconomic Challenges**: Migrant workers often face issues like inadequate access to healthcare, limited job security, and exclusion from social safety nets. The *Inter-State Migrant Workmen Act* aims to protect migrant workers' rights, but enforcement remains inconsistent. Additionally, language and cultural differences can make integration challenging, leading to social tensions in urban areas.

Government Initiatives for Migrant Welfare

Recognizing the importance and challenges of migrant labour, the government has introduced

various initiatives aimed at supporting and protecting migrant workers:

1. **One Nation, One Ration Card**: This scheme allows migrant workers and their families to access subsidized food grains under the Public Distribution System (PDS) across state borders. As of 2023, the scheme covers over 80% of the migrant population, providing essential food

security for families dependent on remittances.

2. **Affordable Rental Housing Complexes (ARHCs)**: Launched under the *Pradhan Mantri Awas Yojana (PMAY)*, ARHCs aim to provide affordable housing for urban migrants and poor populations. By creating safe, accessible living spaces, this initiative helps address the housing challenges faced by migrant workers.
3. **Skill Development Programs**: Programs like *Deen Dayal Upadhyaya Grameen Kaushalya Yojana (DDU-GKY)* focus on training rural youth, equipping them with skills that increase their employability in both rural and urban sectors. As of the latest data, over 1 million young people from rural areas have been trained, many of whom seek employment in cities.

In Summary The dynamics of migrant labour reflect the socioeconomic contrasts between India's rural and urban regions. While migration offers individuals opportunities to improve their livelihoods, it also brings both positive and challenging effects to local economies. For rural areas, migration provides economic support through remittances but can reduce labour availability for agriculture. In urban areas, migrant labour is crucial for industrial and service sectors but places pressure on resources and infrastructure. Government initiatives focused on food security, housing, and skill development aim to address these challenges and support the welfare of migrant workers.

Review Questions

Q1. Explain in Detail

1. Discuss the different sources of livelihood in rural and urban societies, and explain their significance in shaping the economy.
2. Analyze the role of artisans and entrepreneurs in rural and urban economies. How do their contributions impact local development?
3. Evaluate the importance of rural/urban markets in sustaining livelihoods and promoting economic growth.
4. Explain the concept of migrant labor. How does migration for work impact both rural and urban economies?
5. Discuss the role and challenges faced by local self-governments in improving the livelihood of communities in rural and urban areas.

Q2. Short Notes:

1. Importance of non-farm livelihoods in rural areas.
2. Role of Self-help Groups in rural economic development.
3. Differences between rural and urban livelihoods.
4. Challenges faced by migrant labor in India.
5. Key functions of local self-government in rural development.

Objective Questions

1. Multiple Choice Questions (MCQs)

1. What is the primary goal of subsistence farming?

   a) Maximizing profit
   b) Growing crops for the market
   c) Meeting the food needs of the farmer's household
   d) Exporting crops abroad
   Answer: c) Meeting the food needs of the farmer's household

2. Which of the following is a government initiative aimed at supporting traditional artisan industries?

   a) Ayushman Bharat
   b) MGNREGA
   c) Skill India Mission
   d) SFURTI
   Answer: d) SFURTI

3. The term "push factors" in migration refers to:

   a) Factors that attract people to urban areas
   b) Factors that force people to leave rural areas
   c) Reasons people choose not to migrate
   d) Urban job opportunities
   Answer: b) Factors that force people to leave rural areas

4. Which of the following is NOT typically considered a non-farm livelihood?

   a) Handloom weaving

b) Pottery
c) Crop farming
d) Small retail shops
Answer: c) Crop farming

5. Which scheme allows migrant workers to access subsidized food grains across state borders?

a) PM Awaas Yojana
b) One Nation, One Ration Card
c) Jal Jeevan Mission
d) Atma Nirbhar Bharat
Answer: b) One Nation, One Ration Card

6. MGNREGA was launched to provide:

a) Free healthcare
b) Employment guarantees in rural areas
c) Educational scholarships
d) Food subsidies
Answer: b) Employment guarantees in rural areas

7. Urban entrepreneurship is primarily associated with:

a) Agricultural processing
b) Service and technology industries
c) Fishing and forestry
d) Rural markets
Answer: b) Service and technology industries

8. Which of the following is a "pull factor" for migration to cities?

a) Low wages in rural areas
b) Higher educational opportunities
c) Limited healthcare in rural areas
d) None of the above
Answer: b) Higher educational opportunities

9. "Beti Bachao, Beti Padhao" is a program focused on:

    a) Rural employment
    b) Girl child education and welfare
    c) Building rural roads
    d) Providing sanitation facilities
    Answer: b) Girl child education and welfare

10. What is the main focus of the Jal Jeevan Mission?

    a) Providing internet access in rural areas
    b) Providing clean drinking water
    c) Building rural schools
    d) Promoting sanitation
    Answer: b) Providing clean drinking water

11. Which type of farming focuses on large-scale crop production for sale?

    a) Subsistence farming
    b) Organic farming
    c) Commercial farming
    d) Cooperative farming
    Answer: c) Commercial farming

12. Which scheme aims to provide affordable rental housing for migrant labour?

    a) PM Awaas Yojana
    b) Affordable Rental Housing Complexes (ARHCs)
    c) National Rural Livelihood Mission
    d) Swachh Bharat Mission
    Answer: b) Affordable Rental Housing Complexes (ARHCs)

13. Which program focuses on rural skill development for employment?

    a) NRLM
    b) DDU-GKY
    c) Swachh Bharat Mission

d) PMJDY
Answer: b) DDU-GKY

14. Which of the following is a common challenge faced by artisans?

a) High agricultural output
b) Lack of traditional skills
c) Competition from factory-made goods
d) Access to healthcare
Answer: c) Competition from factory-made goods

15. In urban areas, migrant labour predominantly works in:

a) Agricultural production
b) Construction and manufacturing
c) Tourism and hospitality
d) Mining
Answer: b) Construction and manufacturing

16. Which of these factors affects agricultural productivity?

a) Internet access
b) Access to modern technology
c) Political stability
d) Road infrastructure
Answer: b) Access to modern technology

17. The One Nation, One Ration Card scheme is primarily designed for:

a) Urban entrepreneurs
b) Farmers
c) Migrant workers
d) School children
Answer: c) Migrant workers

18. Skill India Mission primarily aims to:

a) Build roads in rural areas

b) Train individuals for employment opportunities
c) Increase crop productivity
d) Develop irrigation systems
Answer: b) Train individuals for employment opportunities

19. Which of the following supports rural self-help groups?

a) SFURTI
b) Atma Nirbhar Bharat
c) Skill India Mission
d) Gram Panchayat Planning
Answer: a) SFURTI

20. The primary role of remittances in rural economies is to:

a) Finance urban businesses
b) Replace agricultural income
c) Provide a secondary income source
d) Develop new cities
Answer: c) Provide a secondary income source

2. State the following statements are True or False.

1. Commercial farming aims to meet only the farmer's household food needs. **(False)**
2. Artisans face challenges such as limited market reach and lack of modern tools. **(True)**
3. MGNREGA is a program focused on urban employment. **(False)**
4. Migration from rural to urban areas often reduces the agricultural labour force in rural regions. **(True)**
5. Subsistence farming involves large-scale production for the market. **(False)**
6. The Skill India Mission provides vocational training to rural youth. **(True)**
7. SFURTI is a scheme for urban technology startups. **(False)**
8. The "One Nation, One Ration Card" scheme is meant for providing healthcare to rural residents. **(False)**
9. The Ayushman Bharat scheme focuses on universal healthcare. **(True)**

10. Remittances from migrant workers are an important income source in rural areas. **(True)**

15. Migration can lead to increased demand on urban resources like housing and sanitation. **(True)**
16. Jal Jeevan Mission is aimed at providing internet access in rural areas. **(False)**
17. Beti Bachao, Beti Padhao focuses on empowering girl children. **(True)**
18. Rural artisans have no issues with competition from factory-made goods. **(False)**
19. Push factors are reasons that attract individuals to new locations. **(False)**

16. Rural areas have ample modern tools for traditional artisans. **(False)**
17. Urban entrepreneurship is limited to agriculture-related businesses. **(False)**
18. Deen Dayal Upadhyaya Grameen Kaushalya Yojana aims to improve rural sanitation. **(False)**
19. Higher wages in cities are a pull factor for migration. **(True)**
20. SFURTI aims to modernize and support traditional industries. **(True)**

CHAPTER TWO

Local Institutions

Objective: This chapter introduces students to the essential local institutions that govern and support communities, with a focus on rural and urban areas. These institutions — including local self-governments, Self-Help Groups, and administrative bodies — play crucial roles in community development, resource management, and policy implementation.

2.1 Introduction to Local Institutions

Local institutions are essential intermediaries that connect citizens with the state, facilitating communication and decision-making at the community level. They enhance citizen participation by providing platforms for public engagement, enabling individuals to voice their needs and priorities, thereby fostering transparency and accountability in governance. These institutions promote sustainable development tailored to local contexts by assessing resources and social dynamics, which empowers communities to adopt practices that balance ecological concerns with economic growth. Comprising structures like local self-governments, self-help groups (SHGs), and community-based organizations (CBOs), local institutions play a crucial role in service delivery, resource mobilization, conflict resolution, and capacity building, ultimately contributing to the empowerment and development of grassroots communities.

2.2 Local Self-Government and Panchayati Raj

Local self-government in India is designed to empower communities to manage their affairs through elected representatives, ensuring that governance is decentralized and more responsive to local needs. This system is primarily organized through the **Panchayati Raj** framework in rural areas and municipal corporations in urban settings.

Panchayati Raj System

1. **Decentralization of Governance:**

Established through the 73rd Amendment to the Indian Constitution in 1992, the Panchayati Raj system was designed to decentralize governance and empower rural communities. It aims to enhance grassroots participation in decision-making processes and strengthen democracy at the local level.

1. **Three Tiers:**

The Panchayati Raj system consists of three tiers:

Gram Panchayat (Village Level): The basic unit of the Panchayati Raj system, the Gram Panchayat is responsible for local administration in villages. It comprises elected representatives from the village assembly (Gram Sabha), who serve for a five-year term.

Panchayat Samiti (Block Level): This tier coordinates the efforts of several Gram Panchayats within a block, focusing on development planning and implementation. It acts as a link between the Gram Panchayat and the Zilla Parishad.

Zilla Parishad (District Level): The highest tier at the district level, the Zilla Parishad oversees the overall development of the district. It is responsible for formulating policies and ensuring the implementation of programs initiated by the state government.

3. **Responsibilities:**

Local self-governments in the Panchayati Raj system have a wide array of responsibilities, including:

Maintaining Village Infrastructure: This includes the construction and upkeep of roads, irrigation systems, and public facilities.

Implementing Welfare Schemes: Gram Panchayats are tasked with implementing government schemes related to health, education, and rural development, such as the Mahatma Gandhi National Rural Employment Guarantee Act (MGNREGA) and the National Rural Livelihood Mission (NRLM).

Promoting Education and Healthcare Services: They play a pivotal role in promoting literacy and ensuring access to healthcare facilities by coordinating with government health programs.

4. **Key Functionaries:**

The **Sarpanch**, elected by the Gram Sabha, serves as the head of the Gram Panchayat. The Sarpanch has significant authority and responsibilities, coordinating local governance activities, chairing meetings, and representing the village in higher administrative forums. As of 2022, there are over 250,000 Gram Panchayats across India, showcasing the scale of local governance.

Municipal Corporations and Councils

1. **Urban Administration:**

In urban areas, municipal corporations handle city administration, managing essential services like water supply, sanitation, waste management, and urban planning. Municipal governance was formalized through the 74th Amendment to the Constitution in 1992, which aimed to enhance urban local governance.

2. **Structure and Functioning:**

Municipal corporations are headed by a **Mayor**, who is elected by the councilors representing different city wards. These councilors are responsible for addressing local issues and ensuring effective delivery of municipal services. As of 2022, there are approximately 1,500 municipalities in India, including municipal corporations, nagar panchayats, and town councils.

3. **Responsibilities:**

Municipalities aim to address urban development issues such as housing, public transportation, infrastructure development, and waste management. They regulate construction activities, enforce building codes, and ensure compliance with safety standards.

Role in Development

1. **Implementation of National and State Programs:**

Local self-governments play a critical role in implementing various national and state programs at the local level. They adapt these programs to meet community-specific needs, ensuring that development initiatives are relevant and effective. For instance, local bodies have been instrumental in implementing the Swachh Bharat Mission, which aims to achieve a clean and open defecation-free India.

2. **Fostering Community Engagement:**

By giving citizens a voice in decision-making and development processes, local self-governments foster community engagement and empowerment. Initiatives like participatory budgeting allow community members to prioritize projects based on their needs, thus enhancing the overall effectiveness of local governance.

3. **Data and Impact:**

According to the Ministry of Panchayati Raj, as of 2020, over 14 million representatives are involved in the Panchayati Raj system across India. The active participation of local governments has been linked to improved service delivery and increased accountability in governance.

In conclusion, local self-government and the Panchayati Raj system are integral to India's democratic framework, ensuring that governance is more responsive and aligned with the needs of local communities. Through decentralized structures, local institutions play a significant role in the development and empowerment of rural and urban areas, driving progress and fostering sustainable growth.

2.3 Self-Help Groups (SHGs)

Self-Help Groups (SHGs) are community-based organizations that empower members primarily women by promoting savings, providing access to credit, and facilitating collective decision-making. These groups are pivotal in enhancing financial inclusion and fostering entrepreneurship, particularly in rural areas.

Formation and Objectives

- **Composition and Structure:** SHGs usually consist of 10 to 20 members from similar socio-economic backgrounds. The primary aim is to pool resources by contributing small amounts of money into a common fund, which is then utilized for:

Low-Interest Loans: Members can borrow from this fund at minimal interest rates to meet their financial needs or invest in small businesses.

Business Ventures: The pooled resources can be directed toward starting or expanding small enterprises, thereby promoting local economic development.

- **Objectives:**

Financial Inclusion: SHGs aim to include marginalized communities in the formal banking system, allowing them access to savings accounts, loans, and insurance.

Entrepreneurship Skills: Members are encouraged to develop skills related to business management, financial literacy, and marketing, thereby enhancing their employability and income potential.

Livelihood Improvement: By providing financial and social support, SHGs aim to improve the overall livelihood of members and their families.

Role in Rural Development

- **Poverty Alleviation:**

SHGs significantly contribute to reducing poverty levels in rural areas by providing access to credit where traditional banking facilities are scarce. This financial support helps members meet immediate needs and invest in income-generating activities.

- **Women's Empowerment:**

Empowering women is a critical aspect of SHGs. Members often gain financial independence, improve their decision-making power within the household, and actively participate in community affairs. This empowerment extends beyond financial aspects to include social and political dimensions.

- **Collabouration with NGOs and Government:**

Many SHGs partner with Non-Governmental Organizations (NGOs) and government initiatives to enhance their capacity. This collabouration can include:

Skills Training: Workshops on various skills such as tailoring, handicrafts, and agriculture to improve members' productivity.

Marketing Support: Assistance in marketing products produced by SHG members, often through exhibitions and online platforms.

Case Study: National Rural Livelihood Mission (NRLM)

- **Overview:**

Launched in 2011 by the Government of India, the National Rural Livelihood Mission (NRLM) aims to promote self-employment and organization of rural poor into SHGs. Its mission is to reduce poverty by promoting self-reliance through skill development and financial inclusion.

- **Support Mechanisms:**

Skill Development Programs: NRLM provides training programs in various trades, equipping women with the necessary skills to enhance their employability and entrepreneurship.

Financial Inclusion Initiatives: NRLM facilitates access to bank credit and other financial services, enabling SHGs to leverage their collective strength.

- **Impact:**

According to the NRLM's 2023 report, over 8.5 crore households have been organized into SHGs across India, with a focus on empowering women. This initiative has led to increased household incomes and improved standards of living.

Real-Time Data: As of 2023, the average monthly income of SHG members has increased by 25% since the inception of the NRLM. The program has also enhanced the skills of over 2.5 crore rural women, leading to increased participation in the workforce.

2.4 Local Administration

Local administration plays a crucial role in governance by managing public services, enforcing laws, and implementing policies at the grassroots level. It serves as a bridge between the government and the community, ensuring that the needs of citizens are met effectively and efficiently.

Administrative Structure

- **Rural Administration:**

In rural areas, local administration is primarily managed by officials like the **Talathi** (village revenue officer) and the **Block Development Officer** (BDO). The Talathi is responsible for maintaining land records, collecting revenue, and assisting in the implementation of government schemes at the village level. The BDO oversees the developmental activities of a block, coordinating various government programs and ensuring that they are executed properly.

- **Urban Administration:**

In urban settings, local governance is typically overseen by officials such as the **Municipal Commissioner** and the **Revenue Officer**. The Municipal Commissioner manages the municipal corporation, ensuring the delivery of essential services like waste management, public health, and urban planning. The Revenue Officer focuses on property tax collection, land use regulations, and maintaining land records within the city.

- **Responsibilities:**

Both rural and urban local administrations are tasked with maintaining land records, collecting taxes, and overseeing welfare programs. They also play a vital role in disaster management and emergency response, especially during natural calamities.

Functions of Local Administration

- **Public Service Delivery:**

Local administrations are responsible for ensuring that essential services such as healthcare, education, sanitation, and water supply are accessible to all citizens. They implement programs like the **Pradhan Mantri Awas Yojana** (PMAY), which aims to provide affordable housing to the urban poor, and **Swachh Bharat Mission**, which focuses on sanitation and hygiene.

- **Regulatory Role:**

They also have a significant regulatory function, which includes enforcing laws related to public safety, health codes, and building regulations. For instance, local administrations ensure compliance with the **Environmental Protection Act** by monitoring industries and urban developments to prevent environmental degradation.

- **Welfare Programs:**

Local administrations coordinate and implement various national and state welfare schemes. **Mahatma Gandhi National Rural Employment Guarantee Act** (MGNREGA) provides guaranteed employment in rural areas, while **Ayushman Bharat** aims to provide health coverage to economically vulnerable populations. As of 2023, MGNREGA has generated over 220 crore person-days of employment, showcasing the significant role of local administration in poverty alleviation and job creation.

Challenges Faced

- **Budget Constraints:**

Local administrations often operate under limited budgets, which hinders their ability to provide adequate public services. The **13th Finance Commission** has recommended increasing the share of local bodies in the state revenue to enhance their financial capabilities, but many local administrations still struggle to meet the demands of their communities.

- **Staff Shortages and Bureaucratic Delays:**

There are often staff shortages within local administration, leading to delays in service delivery and a backlog of pending applications for various services. For example, the average processing time for land record updates can extend from weeks to several months, frustrating citizens and impacting their livelihoods.

- **Bridging Policy and Practice:**

One of the most significant challenges is bridging the gap between policy and practice. While various schemes are launched at the national level, their implementation often falters at the local level due to lack of awareness, poor coordination, and bureaucratic red tape. Issues of accountability and transparency further exacerbate these challenges, leading to public distrust in local governance.

Conclusion

Local administration serves as the backbone of governance in India, playing a pivotal role in delivering essential services and implementing welfare programs. Despite the challenges faced, including budget constraints, staff shortages, and the gap between policy and practice, local administrations remain crucial for fostering community development and improving the quality of life for citizens. Real-time data and ongoing government initiatives highlight the need for continuous support and reform to strengthen local governance, ensuring that it effectively meets the needs of the population.

2.5 Community Participation in Local Institutions

Community participation in local institutions is essential for fostering effective governance and ensuring that the needs and priorities of citizens are addressed. Active engagement from the community not only enhances the legitimacy of local governance but also empowers citizens to take an active role in shaping their environment.

Importance of Community Engagement

- **Responsive Governance:**

Local institutions thrive when communities actively engage in governance processes. Citizen participation ensures that local government actions reflect the actual needs and priorities of the community. By involving citizens in decision-making, local administrations can better identify and address issues that matter most to the residents, leading to more tailored and effective policies.

- **Empowerment and Ownership:**

When communities are involved in governance, they feel a sense of ownership over local initiatives. This empowerment leads to increased civic responsibility and encourages citizens to actively participate in community development efforts. For instance, community-driven projects often see higher levels of participation and support, as residents are more likely to engage with initiatives they helped create.

- **Building Trust:**

Regular engagement between local institutions and community members fosters trust in governance. When citizens see their input being valued and acted upon, it enhances their confidence in local authorities. This trust is crucial for ensuring compliance with local regulations and supporting community-led initiatives.

Gram Sabha and Ward Meetings

- **Platforms for Engagement:** In rural areas, **Gram Sabha** meetings serve as a crucial platform for community participation. These gatherings bring together members of the village to discuss local governance issues, budget allocations, infrastructure needs, and grievances. Similarly, in urban areas, **Ward meetings** provide an avenue for residents to voice their concerns and suggestions directly to local officials.
- **Transparency and Accountability:** Regular meetings encourage transparency and accountability in local governance. By providing a space for open discussions, Gram Sabha and Ward meetings enable citizens to scrutinize the actions of their elected representatives and local authorities. This oversight is essential for holding officials accountable for their decisions and expenditures.
- **Empowering Voices:** These meetings empower marginalized voices within the community, including women, the elderly, and the economically disadvantaged. By ensuring that all segments of society have the opportunity to participate, local institutions can address inequalities and ensure more inclusive decision-making.
- **Real-Time Data and Impact:** According to a 2022 report by the Ministry of Panchayati Raj, there has been a significant increase in the number of Gram Sabha meetings across India, with over 1.5 lakh meetings held annually. These meetings have led to increased community engagement in local development projects, resulting in improved infrastructure and services in many rural areas. Community participation in local institutions is vital for effective governance and sustainable development. By fostering engagement through platforms like Gram Sabha and Ward meetings, local administrations can ensure that their actions are responsive to the needs of the community. This participatory approach not only enhances transparency and accountability but also empowers citizens to take ownership of their local governance, leading

to stronger, more resilient communities. The real-time data highlighting the growth of community engagement initiatives underscores the positive impact of participatory governance on local development outcomes.

Review Question

Q1. Long Answer Questions:

1. Discuss the role of local self-governments and the Panchayati Raj system in empowering rural communities and improving governance in India.
2. Analyze the structure and functioning of municipal corporations in urban areas. How do they address key urban issues such as housing, sanitation, and waste management?
3. Explain the concept of Self-Help Groups (SHGs) and their impact on poverty alleviation, women's empowerment, and rural development.
4. Evaluate the challenges faced by local administrations in rural and urban areas, particularly in terms of budget constraints, staff shortages, and bureaucratic delays.
5. Discuss the importance of community participation in local institutions. How do platforms like Gram Sabha and Ward meetings foster transparency, accountability, and inclusive decision-making?

Q2. Short Notes:

1. Role of Gram Panchayat in rural governance.
2. Key objectives of the National Rural Livelihood Mission for SHGs.
3. Functions of the Municipal Commissioner in urban administration.
4. Benefits of community participation in local governance.
5. Responsibilities of the Zilla Parishad in the Panchayati Raj system.

1.Multiple Choice Questions (MCQs)

1. **What is the primary purpose of local self-government in India?**

   A) Centralized governance
   B) Decentralized administration
   C) National control
   D) International relations

Answer: B) Decentralized administration

2. Which amendment to the Indian Constitution established the Panchayati Raj system?

A) 61st Amendment

B) 73rd Amendment

C) 74th Amendment

D) 86th Amendment

Answer: B) 73rd Amendment

3. **Which of the following is NOT a tier of the Panchayati Raj system?**

A) Gram Panchayat

B) Zilla Parishad

C) Rajya Sabha

D) Panchayat Samiti

Answer: C) Rajya Sabha

4. **The head of a Gram Panchayat is known as the:**

A) Mayor

B) Sarpanch

C) Ward Councilor

D) Block Development Officer

Answer: B) Sarpanch

5. **Municipal corporations primarily manage:**

A) Rural infrastructure

B) Urban administration

C) Agricultural services

D) Environmental conservation

Answer: B) Urban administration

6. **Who is responsible for implementing welfare schemes at the village level?**

A) Zilla Parishad

B) Panchayat Samiti

C) Gram Panchayat
D) State Government
Answer: C) Gram Panchayat

7. **The Mayor is elected from which of the following?**

A) State Legislature
B) Municipal Councilors
C) Gram Sabha
D) District Collector
Answer: B) Municipal Councilors

8. **Which of the following acts as a link between Gram Panchayats and the Zilla Parishad?**

A) Gram Sabha
B) Panchayat Samiti
C) Municipal Council
D) Self-Help Groups
Answer: B) Panchayat Samiti

9. **The Zilla Parishad operates at which level of governance?**

A) Village Level
B) Block Level
C) District Level
D) State Level
Answer: C) District Level

10. **Local self-governments help implement programs at which level?**

A) International
B) National
C) Local
D) State
Answer: C) Local

11. **Which of the following is a function of local self-governments?**

A) Enforcing national laws
B) Managing local infrastructure
C) Conducting international trade
D) Overseeing central policies
Answer: B) Managing local infrastructure

12. **Which institution is responsible for urban planning in municipalities?**

A) Gram Panchayat
B) Zilla Parishad
C) Municipal Corporation
D) Panchayat Samiti
Answer: C) Municipal Corporation

13. **What is a key feature of the Panchayati Raj system?**

A) Centralized control
B) Direct elections
C) Bureaucratic governance
D) Authoritarian leadership
Answer: B) Direct elections

14. **The Gram Sabha consists of:**

A) Elected representatives
B) All registered voters in the village
C) Government officials
D) Members of the Zilla Parishad
Answer: B) All registered voters in the village

15. **Which of the following is true regarding the Panchayati Raj system?**

A) It is only for urban areas
B) It promotes grassroots democracy
C) It eliminates local governance
D) It is a federal system of governance
Answer: B) It promotes grassroots democracy

16. **How often are elections held for the Panchayati Raj system?**

    A) Every year
    B) Every two years
    C) Every five years
    D) Every ten years
    Answer: C) Every five years

17. **Which program aims to achieve a clean and open defecation-free India?**

    A) Beti Bachao Beti Padhao
    B) Swachh Bharat Mission
    C) Skill India Mission
    D) MGNREGA
    Answer: B) Swachh Bharat Mission

18. **Local self-governments provide services such as:**

    A) Defense and foreign affairs
    B) Water supply and sanitation
    C) National security
    D) International relations
    Answer: B) Water supply and sanitation

19. **What is one challenge faced by local self-governments?**

    A) Excessive authority
    B) Lack of community participation
    C) Overfunding
    D) Centralized control
    Answer: B) Lack of community participation

20. **Local self-governments are crucial for:**

    A) Global trade
    B) Local development
    C) National defense

D) International diplomacy

Answer: B) Local development

2. State the following statemen are true or false.

1. The Panchayati Raj system consists of three tiers: Gram Panchayat, Panchayat Samiti, and Zilla Parishad. **(True)**
2. The Sarpanch is elected by the Zilla Parishad. **(False)**
3. Municipal corporations manage rural infrastructure. **(False)**
4. The Gram Sabha consists of all registered voters in the village. **(True)**
5. The Mayor is the head of a Gram Panchayat. **(False)**
6. Local self-governments help implement national programs at the local level. **(True)**
7. The Panchayat Samiti operates at the village level. **(False)**
8. The Zilla Parishad is responsible for overseeing district-level governance. **(True)**
9. Elections for local self-governments are held every two years. **(False)**
10. Local self-governments do not have any role in service delivery. **(False)**
11. The 74th Amendment to the Constitution deals with urban local governance. **(True)**
12. The Panchayati Raj system promotes centralized decision-making. **(False)**
13. Self-Help Groups (SHGs) are part of the local self-government structure. **(True)**
14. Local self-governments have the authority to regulate construction activities. **(True)**
15. The Gram Panchayat is the highest level of local self-government. **(False)**
16. Municipal councils handle city administration in urban areas. **(True)**
17. The Sarpanch is a bureaucratic position with no electoral process. **(False)**
18. Local self-governments are essential for fostering grassroots democracy. **(True)**
19. Local self-governments can only implement state-level programs. **(False)**
20. The Panchayati Raj system was established in 1947. **(False)**

CHAPTER THREE

National Development Programs

Objective: This chapter introduces students to India's major development programs and their role in enhancing socio-economic conditions. These programs cover areas like education, health, infrastructure, employment, and skill development, contributing to the nation's goal of sustainable and inclusive growth.

3.1 Introduction to National Development Programs

India's development programs are essential frameworks designed to tackle the unique challenges faced by its diverse population across both rural and urban landscapes. These initiatives aim to enhance living standards, promote sustainable economic growth, and empower citizens by addressing key areas such as poverty alleviation, education, healthcare, and infrastructure development. By implementing targeted strategies and leveraging local resources, these programs not only aim to uplift marginalized communities but also contribute to the overall national development agenda. As students explore these initiatives, they gain valuable insights into the interplay between government policies and community welfare, ultimately understanding how effective governance can lead to tangible improvements in people's lives.

3.2 Key National Programs and Initiatives

3.2.1 Education Initiatives

Sarva Shiksha Abhiyan (SSA): Launched in 2001, the Sarva Shiksha Abhiyan aims to achieve universal elementary education by providing free and compulsory education for children aged 6 to 14 years. The program's key objectives include building schools, recruiting qualified teachers, and raising awareness to minimize dropout rates, particularly among marginalized communities. As of 2023, the Gross Enrollment Ratio (GER) in primary education has reached approximately **96%**, reflecting the success of SSA in increasing access to education. However, challenges remain in ensuring quality education and reducing the dropout rates among disadvantaged groups, necessitating continuous efforts and monitoring.

BetiBachao,BetiPadhao: This initiative, launched in 2015, addresses gender disparities in education and promotes the empowerment of girls. By focusing on reducing female feticide and improving the enrollment and retention of girls in schools, particularly in regions with skewed gender ratios, the program has made significant strides. As of 2023, the female literacy rate has improved to **70.99%**, with the initiative contributing to the enrollment of over **20 million** girls in schools across the country. Community awareness campaigns and targeted scholarships for girls have played a crucial role in these achievements.

3.2.2 Health and Sanitation Programs

Ayushman Bharat: Launched in 2018, Ayushman Bharat is recognized as the world's largest government-funded healthcare program, providing health insurance coverage of up to **₹5 lakh** per family per year for economically vulnerable families. By 2023, the program has covered over **13 crore families**, significantly improving access to healthcare services. The initiative aims to alleviate the financial burden of medical expenses on low-income households and enhance the quality of healthcare through the establishment of Health and Wellness Centers across the country.

Swachh Bharat Abhiyan: Initiated in 2014, this program aims to eliminate open defecation and improve sanitation facilities across urban and rural India. It has had a transformative impact on hygiene practices, with over **11 crore toilets** constructed under the initiative by 2023. Efforts under Swachh Bharat include awareness campaigns that educate communities about hygiene practices, as well as setting up waste management systems to promote cleanliness. The program has contributed to a significant decrease in waterborne diseases and improved public health outcomes.

3.2.3 Housing and Infrastructure Development

PradhanMantriAwaas Yojana (PMAY): Launched in 2015, PMAY aims to provide affordable housing for all by constructing homes equipped with basic amenities for economically weaker sections. As of 2023, over **1.2 crore houses** have been sanctioned under PMAY, with nearly **70 lakh houses** completed. The initiative focuses on achieving "Housing for All" through both urban and rural housing schemes, addressing the growing need for adequate shelter in India, particularly in rapidly urbanizing regions.

Jal Jeevan Mission: This initiative, launched in 2019, aims to ensure access to safe and adequate drinking water for rural households through tap water connections. The program focuses on water conservation and sustainable resource management, addressing the water scarcity issues faced by many rural communities. By 2023, the mission has successfully provided tap water connections to over **9 crore rural households**, significantly improving the quality of life and health outcomes in these areas.

3.2.4 Employment and Skill Development Programs

SkillIndiaMission: Launched in 2015, the Skill India Mission aims to enhance employability by providing vocational training to youth, making them job-ready across various sectors. As of 2023, more than **1.5 crore individuals** have undergone skill training, covering a diverse range of sectors, including IT, healthcare, and manufacturing. The mission emphasizes skill certification, entrepreneurship development, and skill upgrading in emerging sectors to meet the demands of a dynamic job market.

Mahatma Gandhi National Rural Employment Guarantee Act (MGNREGA):
MGNREGA guarantees 100 days of paid work per year to rural households, focusing on labour-intensive projects such as road construction, irrigation, and water conservation. As of 2023, the scheme has benefited over **12 crore households**, providing a financial safety net for rural families while enhancing rural infrastructure and resource management. MGNREGA plays a crucial role in empowering rural communities and addressing issues of unemployment.

3.2.5 Livelihood Support and Traditional Industries

National Rural Livelihood Mission(NRLM): NRLM aims to improve rural livelihoods by organizing the poor into Self-Help Groups (SHGs) and linking them to banks for financial support. The program has been instrumental in empowering women through SHGs, promoting small businesses, and enhancing access to credit and skill development. As of 2023, NRLM has formed over **7.2 crore SHGs**, benefiting around **36 crore individuals**, thereby improving financial independence and livelihoods in rural areas.

Scheme of Fundfor Regeneration of Traditional Industries (SFURTI):

SFURTI promotes traditional industries, such as handloom and handicrafts, by supporting artisans and creating sustainable business models. By enhancing the productivity and profitability of these traditional industries, SFURTI not only preserves cultural heritage but also boosts local economies. As of 2023, the scheme has provided financial and technical support to over **1.5 lakh artisans**, ensuring their livelihoods while fostering the growth of traditional crafts.

3.2.6 Self-Reliance and Economic Empowerment

AtmaNirbhar Bharat(Self-Reliant IndiaMission): Introduced in 2020, this initiative aims to boost India's domestic manufacturing and reduce dependency on imports by focusing on sectors such as defense, electronics, and Micro, Small, and Medium Enterprises (MSMEs). The mission encourages entrepreneurship, promotes local products, and increases investment in infrastructure. As of 2023, Atma Nirbhar Bharat has led to the establishment of over **2.5 lakh MSMEs**, significantly contributing to job creation and economic growth in the country. Through various schemes, the government aims to foster an environment of self-reliance and resilience in the Indian economy.

3.3 Program Implementation and Challenges

Despite the positive impact of various national programs and initiatives aimed at enhancing the livelihoods of citizens, several challenges hinder effective implementation:

BudgetConstraints: One of the primary challenges in implementing development programs is the issue of budget constraints. Insufficient funding often limits the reach and effectiveness of these initiatives, particularly in rural and remote areas. Many programs require substantial financial resources for infrastructure development, training, and service delivery. For instance, the budget allocation for the Mahatma Gandhi National Rural Employment Guarantee Act (MGNREGA) has faced cuts in recent years, leading to delays in wage payments and reduced employment opportunities for rural households. According to the Ministry of Finance, the allocation for MGNREGA was reduced from ₹61,500 crores in 2020-21 to ₹73,000 crores in 2021-22, which may not adequately cover the rising demand for work.

AwarenessandAccessibility: Another significant hurdle is the lack of awareness among communities regarding the benefits and eligibility criteria of various government programs. Many potential beneficiaries remain uninformed about available initiatives, which limits their participation and access to support. For example, despite the benefits of the Ayushman Bharat program, studies have shown that less than **30%** of eligible families are aware of the scheme, which hampers its impact on improving healthcare access. Awareness campaigns must be strengthened to ensure that communities are well-informed about their rights and the support available to them.

AdministrativeHurdles: Administrative hurdles also pose a challenge in the timely delivery and monitoring of these initiatives. Bureaucratic delays, lack of coordination among departments, and inadequate resources can slow down the implementation process. For example, delays in fund disbursement for the Pradhan Mantri Awaas Yojana (PMAY) can hinder the construction of homes, ultimately affecting beneficiaries who rely on this support for stable housing. Streamlining administrative processes and enhancing inter-departmental coordination can help mitigate these delays.

Monitoring and Accountability: Ensuring transparency and accountability in program implementation is crucial for achieving effective outcomes. There are often concerns regarding the misuse of funds, corruption, and lack of oversight, which can undermine the effectiveness of these initiatives. For instance, irregularities in the distribution of benefits under the National Rural Livelihood Mission (NRLM) have been reported, where funds intended for Self-Help Groups (SHGs) have been misappropriated. Establishing robust monitoring mechanisms and promoting citizen engagement in the oversight of these programs can enhance accountability and ensure that resources are used effectively.

In summary, while government programs are essential for supporting national growth and improving livelihoods, addressing these challenges is vital to maximize their impact and ensure that benefits reach the intended populations. Strengthening financial allocations, raising awareness, streamlining administration, and enhancing monitoring mechanisms are key steps in overcoming these obstacles.

3.4 Case Studies of Success and Impact

1. Ayushman Bharat in Rural India: The Ayushman Bharat initiative has had a transformative impact on healthcare access for low-income families in rural areas of India. Before the implementation of this program, many families were unable to afford essential medical treatments, often leading to catastrophic health expenditures that plunged them into debt.

For instance, a case study from Madhya Pradesh illustrates this impact vividly. A family of five, previously relying on local healers due to financial constraints, sought treatment for a critical illness after enrolling in the Ayushman Bharat scheme. With coverage for hospitalization costs, they accessed quality healthcare in a nearby government hospital. Post-treatment, their health outcomes improved significantly, allowing the breadwinner to return to work promptly. The family reported a reduction in medical expenses, shifting from out-of-pocket expenditures that often led to financial strain to being fully covered by the insurance scheme. According to data from the National Health Authority, over **10 crore** families have benefited from Ayushman Bharat, highlighting a significant reduction in financial barriers to healthcare access.

2. MGNREGAand Employment Security: The Mahatma Gandhi National Rural Employment Guarantee Act (MGNREGA) has played a crucial role in providing employment security to rural families, particularly in regions that experience seasonal unemployment. This scheme guarantees **100 days** of wage employment per year, which has been a lifeline for many.

In Bihar, for example, a study of a village affected by agricultural seasonal fluctuations revealed that families relied on MGNREGA work during off-seasons. One such family, consisting of six members, participated in MGNREGA projects like road construction and water conservation. The guaranteed wages helped them maintain their livelihoods, preventing distress migration to urban areas in search of work. The initiative not only provided financial security but also contributed to better rural infrastructure, including improved roads and irrigation facilities. Data from the Ministry of Rural Development indicates that MGNREGA has created over **30 crore** person-days of employment, significantly enhancing rural livelihoods and community resilience.

3. SkillIndia in Urban Centers: Skill India has emerged as a key initiative to enhance the employability of youth in urban areas, particularly in fast-growing sectors such as Information Technology (IT) and manufacturing. Through various vocational training programs, the initiative aims to equip the youth with relevant skills to meet market demands.

For instance, a case study conducted in Bengaluru highlighted the effectiveness of Skill India training centers in preparing graduates for the tech industry. One participant, a young woman who underwent training in software development, secured a position in a leading IT firm after completing her course. Graduates reported increased employment opportunities and a notable growth in their income levels, often doubling their previous earnings. According to the Ministry of Skill Development and

Entrepreneurship, over **1.5 crore** individuals have been trained under the Skill India initiative, underscoring its success in fostering job readiness and economic empowerment.

Review Question

Q1. Long Answer Questions:

1. Discuss the objectives and impact of the Sarva Shiksha Abhiyan (SSA) on the education sector in India, highlighting the challenges faced in achieving universal elementary education.
2. Explain the key features of the Ayushman Bharat scheme and analyze its role in improving healthcare accessibility for economically vulnerable families. Include examples of its success in rural areas.
3. Assess the effectiveness of the Mahatma Gandhi National Rural Employment Guarantee Act (MGNREGA) in providing employment security to rural households. How has it contributed to rural infrastructure development?
4. Describe the Pradhan Mantri Awaas Yojana (PMAY) and its role in addressing the housing needs of economically weaker sections in both urban and rural areas. Discuss the challenges encountered in the implementation of the scheme.
5. Analyze the impact of the Skill India Mission on youth employability, particularly in urban centers. Provide examples of how vocational training has helped individuals secure jobs in various sectors.

Q2. Short Note Questions:

1. Explain the objectives of the Beti Bachao, Beti Padhao initiative and its contribution to female education in India.
2. Describe the goals of the Swachh Bharat Abhiyan and its impact on sanitation and public health.
3. Outline the objectives and outcomes of the Jal Jeevan Mission in providing safe drinking water to rural households.
4. Discuss the significance of the Atma Nirbhar Bharat initiative in promoting self-reliance and economic empowerment in India.
5. Summarize the role of the National Rural Livelihood Mission (NRLM) in improving rural livelihoods through Self-Help Groups (SHGs).

Objective Question

Q1. Multiple-Choice Questions (MCQs) –

1. Which of the following is the primary goal of the Sarva Shiksha Abhiyan (SSA)?

   A) Improve sanitation
   B) Provide universal elementary education
   C) Promote rural employment
   D) Increase agricultural productivity
   Answer: B) Provide universal elementary education

1. Which program is known as the world's largest government-funded healthcare scheme?

   A) Swachh Bharat Abhiyan
   B) Pradhan Mantri Awaas Yojana
   C) Ayushman Bharat
   D) Skill India Mission
   Answer: C) Ayushman Bharat

3. What is the primary objective of the Beti Bachao, Beti Padhao initiative?

   A) Improve healthcare for women
   B) Encourage higher education among girls
   C) Address gender disparities and female feticide
   D) Increase job opportunities for women
   Answer: C) Address gender disparities and female feticide

4. The Swachh Bharat Abhiyan was primarily launched to:

   A) Promote education
   B) Eliminate open defecation and improve sanitation
   C) Provide rural employment
   D) Improve healthcare access
   Answer: B) Eliminate open defecation and improve sanitation

5. Which of the following is NOT a goal of Pradhan Mantri Awaas Yojana (PMAY)?

A) Provide affordable housing
B) Offer healthcare benefits
C) Include basic amenities in housing
D) Ensure housing for economically weaker sections
Answer: B) Offer healthcare benefits

6. The Jal Jeevan Mission aims to:

A) Improve irrigation systems for agriculture
B) Ensure access to safe drinking water
C) Promote skill development among youth
D) Eliminate rural unemployment
Answer: B) Ensure access to safe drinking water

7. Which program guarantees 100 days of wage employment per year for rural households?

A) Skill India Mission
B) Pradhan Mantri Awaas Yojana
C) MGNREGA
D) Atma Nirbhar Bharat
Answer: C) MGNREGA

8. NRLM primarily aims to improve rural livelihoods through:

A) Providing healthcare benefits
B) Offering vocational training
C) Organizing Self-Help Groups (SHGs)
D) Encouraging urban migration
Answer: C) Organizing Self-Help Groups (SHGs)

9. Which initiative is focused on preserving traditional industries like handloom and handicrafts?

A) Skill India Mission
B) Jal Jeevan Mission
C) SFURTI
D) Beti Bachao, Beti Padhao

Answer: C) SFURTI

10. Which level of Panchayati Raj deals with district-level administration?

A) Gram Panchayat
B) Panchayat Samiti
C) Zilla Parishad
D) Gram Sabha
Answer: C) Zilla Parishad

11. Which position heads the Gram Panchayat in a village?

A) Sarpanch
B) Mayor
C) Collector
D) Councilor
Answer: A) Sarpanch

12. Atma Nirbhar Bharat aims to:

A) Improve sanitation
B) Boost India's self-reliance and reduce import dependency
C) Offer employment in urban areas
D) Build houses for the economically weaker sections
Answer: B) Boost India's self-reliance and reduce import dependency

13. Which body primarily administers services like water supply and waste management in urban areas?

A) Panchayat Samiti
B) Gram Sabha
C) Municipal Corporation
D) Zilla Parishad
Answer: C) Municipal Corporation

14. The Skill India Mission focuses on:

A) Providing universal education

B) Offering skill training to youth
C) Building houses
D) Providing healthcare insurance
Answer: B) Offering skill training to youth

15. Which initiative is primarily designed to help rural women through Self-Help Groups (SHGs)?

    A) NRLM
    B) SSA
    C) Beti Bachao, Beti Padhao
    D) PMAY
    Answer: A) NRLM

16. What is the primary focus of the Swachh Bharat Mission?

    A) Access to education
    B) Clean water supply
    C) Improve sanitation and eliminate open defecation
    D) Increase healthcare access
    Answer: C) Improve sanitation and eliminate open defecation

17. Which program focuses on employment generation in rural India?

    A) MGNREGA
    B) PMAY
    C) Beti Bachao, Beti Padhao
    D) Jal Jeevan Mission
    Answer: A) MGNREGA

18. In the Panchayati Raj system, which is the first tier at the village level?

    A) Zilla Parishad
    B) Gram Panchayat
    C) Panchayat Samiti
    D) Municipal Corporation
    Answer: B) Gram Panchayat

19. Which initiative provides financial support for healthcare to low-income families in India?

    A) PMAY
    B) MGNREGA
    C) Ayushman Bharat
    D) Skill India Mission
    Answer: C) Ayushman Bharat

20. Which initiative aims to provide affordable housing to all by 2022?

    A) Jal Jeevan Mission
    B) Pradhan Mantri Awaas Yojana
    C) Beti Bachao, Beti Padhao
    D) MGNREGA
    Answer: B) Pradhan Mantri Awaas Yojana

Q2. State the following statemen are true or false.

1. The Sarva Shiksha Abhiyan focuses on providing universal secondary education. **(False).**
2. Ayushman Bharat is a healthcare initiative to provide free medical treatment to low-income families. **(True)**
3. The primary goal of the Beti Bachao, Beti Padhao program is to address gender disparities. **(True)**
4. Swachh Bharat Abhiyan is primarily focused on housing development. **(False)**
5. PMAY is designed to improve rural sanitation. **(False)**
6. Jal Jeevan Mission aims to provide access to clean drinking water in rural areas. **(True)**
7. MGNREGA guarantees 200 days of employment for rural households. **(False)**
8. NRLM focuses on enhancing rural livelihoods through Self-Help Groups. **(True)**
9. SFURTI is a scheme aimed at regenerating traditional industries. **(True)**
10. The Sarpanch is the head of the Zilla Parishad. **(False)**
11. The Skill India Mission aims to improve employment through vocational training. **(True).**

12. The Municipal Corporation is responsible for handling urban sanitation. **(True)**
13. Atma Nirbhar Bharat is focused on reducing India's reliance on imports. **(True)**
14. The Panchayat Samiti operates at the district level in the Panchayati Raj system. **(False)**
15. Ayushman Bharat provides health insurance to economically weaker sections. **(True)**
16. MGNREGA is designed specifically to improve education access in rural areas. **(False)**
17. Pradhan Mantri Awaas Yojana aims to provide affordable housing. **(True)**
18. The Gram Panchayat operates at the block level in the Panchayati Raj system. **(False)**
19. Beti Bachao, Beti Padhao seeks to reduce female feticide and promote education for girls. **(True)**
20. Skill India Mission is primarily a healthcare program. **(False)**

Question Paper-1 (autonomous Colleges)

Community Engagement Project (Discipline Specific Core Course)
Course Code: COL4CEP
Total Marks: 20
Duration: 1 Hour

Q.1 Attempt any ten out of twelve (Multiple Choice Questions): (10 Marks)

1.Which scheme provides 100 days of guaranteed employment to rural households in India?

a) Pradhan Mantri Awaas Yojana

b) Sarva Shiksha Abhiyan

c) MGNREGA

d) Ayushman Bharat

2.The National Rural Livelihood Mission (NRLM) focuses primarily on:

a) Improving healthcare in urban areas

b) Empowering women through SHGs

c) Developing school infrastructure

d) Providing digital literacy

3.The main purpose of the Swachh Bharat Mission is to:

a) Promote rural employment

b) Improve urban sanitation

c) Provide quality education

d) Encourage sustainable farming

4.The Jal Jeevan Mission aims to:

a) Provide financial aid for rural families

b) Ensure safe drinking water for all households

c) Build low-cost housing

d) Enhance digital literacy in rural areas

5.Self-Help Groups (SHGs) are primarily associated with:

a) Urban development

b) Community-based financial support

c) Governmental policy-making

d) Large industrial projects

6.Which scheme is designed to promote education for girls and reduce the dropout rate?

a) Beti Bachao, Beti Padhao

b) Skill India Mission

c) Atma Nirbhar Bharat

d) Digital India

7.Atma Nirbhar Bharat focuses on:

a) Importing goods from foreign countries

b) Promoting self-sufficiency and local production

c) Providing housing to urban populations

d) Developing rural roads

8.The key objective of Ayushman Bharat is:

a) Rural employment

b) Health insurance coverage for low-income families

c) Free education for children

d) Infrastructure development

9.Which body is responsible for managing elementary education at the local level?

a) Panchayat Samiti

b) Zilla Parishad

c) Sarva Shiksha Abhiyan

d) Municipal Corporation

10.Pradhan Mantri Gram Sadak Yojana focuses on:

a) Urban housing

b) Rural road connectivity

c) Industrial development

d) Healthcare facilities

11.SFURTI is primarily aimed at:

a) Boosting IT industries

b) Revitalizing traditional and artisan industries

c) Developing higher education

d) Promoting urban sanitation

12.The Gram Sabha is a decision-making body for:

a) Central policies

b) Local self-governance in villages

c) National educational programs

d) Health policies

Q.2 Attempt any ten out of twelve (Objective Questions): (10 Marks)

1. The main goal of MGNREGA is to provide guaranteed healthcare.
2. The primary aim of _____ is to provide affordable housing to low-income

families.

3. Beti Bachao, Beti Padhao focuses on the education and welfare of young boys.
4. ____ aims to provide safe drinking water to every rural household.
5. The ____ scheme is focused on providing vocational training to increase employment opportunities.
6. The goal of ____ is to encourage local manufacturing and reduce dependency on imports.

Q2B. Match the following:

1) Skill India - **(i) Vocational training**

2) NRLM - **(ii) Women's SHGs and rural livelihoods**

3) Swachh Bharat Mission - **(iii) Sanitation and cleanliness**

4) Gram Panchayat - **(ii) Local self-government in villages**

5) Zilla Parishad - **(iii) District-level rural administration**

6) Municipal Corporation - **(i) Urban administration**

Question Paper-1 (university Affiliated Colleges)

Community Engagement Project (Discipline Specific Core Course)
Course Code: COL4CEP
Total Marks: 20
Duration: 1 Hour

Q.1 Attempt the following Multiple-Choice Questions (1/2 mark each): (10 Marks)

1. Which of the following is a national development program aimed at improving rural sanitation?

   a) Sarva Shiksha Abhiyan
   b) Ayushman Bharat
   c) Swachh Bharat Mission
   d) Skill India Mission

1. MGNREGA primarily provides:

   a) Education for children
   b) Vocational training
   c) Housing for rural poor
   d) Employment in rural areas

3. Self-help Groups are primarily involved in:

   a) Educational reforms
   b) Employment generation and microfinance
   c) National defense programs
   d) Road construction

4. The main purpose of Beti Bachao, Beti Padhao is:

   a) Eradicate poverty
   b) Promote education and gender equality for girls
   c) Provide healthcare to low-income families
   d) Support traditional industries

5. Atma Nirbhar Bharat's focus is to:

   a) Increase foreign investments
   b) Build urban infrastructure
   c) Promote self-reliance and reduce import dependency
   d) Support education for children

6. Which program is specifically aimed at providing affordable housing?

   a) MGNREGA
   b) Pradhan Mantri Awaas Yojana
   c) Ayushman Bharat
   d) Jal Jeevan Mission

7. A major component of Atma Nirbhar Bharat includes:

   a) Boosting exports
   b) Reducing foreign debt
   c) Promoting local manufacturing
   d) Enhancing literacy

8. The Jal Jeevan Mission aims to provide:

   a) Education facilities
   b) Drinking water supply to rural households
   c) Financial assistance for farmers
   d) Employment opportunities

9. Which body is responsible for primary governance at the district level?

   a) Panchayat Samiti
   b) Gram Sabha
   c) Zilla Parishad
   d) Municipal Corporation

10. The Sarva Shiksha Abhiyan focuses on:

    a) Healthcare for women

b) Elementary education for children
c) Employment generation
d) Promoting industrialization

11. Skill India is an initiative aimed at:

a) Healthcare
b) Water sanitation
c) Vocational training and employment
d) Agricultural development

12. The primary goal of the National Rural Livelihood Mission (NRLM) is to:

a) Provide healthcare in rural areas
b) Support women through SHGs
c) Build rural roads
d) Enhance education in rural areas

13. The Beti Bachao, Beti Padhao program is mainly focused on:

a) Skill development for women
b) Providing jobs for women
c) Gender equality and female empowerment
d) Rural housing

14. The main purpose of a Self-help Group (SHG) is:

a) Promote higher education
b) Support women's economic empowerment
c) Provide healthcare to the elderly
d) Offer housing loans

15. Local administration is managed at the village level by:

a) Zilla Parishad
b) Panchayat Samiti
c) Municipal Corporation
d) Gram Panchayat

16. Which of the following is involved in regenerating traditional industries?

    a) Beti Bachao, Beti Padhao
    b) Skill India Mission
    c) SFURTI
    d) Jal Jeevan Mission

17. Ayushman Bharat is primarily focused on:

    a) Education
    b) Healthcare access for low-income families
    c) Skill development
    d) Employment guarantee

18. The National Rural Livelihood Mission (NRLM) aims to:

    a) Improve rural housing
    b) Promote literacy in urban areas
    c) Enhance rural livelihoods through SHGs
    d) Build road infrastructure

19. Jal Jeevan Mission primarily focuses on:

    a) Urban sanitation
    b) Skill development
    c) Drinking water supply to rural households
    d) Education for girls

20. Which organization works at the village level to manage local administration?

    a) Zilla Parishad
    b) Panchayat Samiti
    c) Gram Panchayat
    d) Municipal Corporation

Q.2 Attempt the following:

A) Explain the terms/concepts (5 Marks)

1. Local self-government
2. Swachh Bharat Mission
3. Self-help Group (SHG)
4. Beti Bachao, Beti Padhao
5. Skill India Mission

B) Answer the following in one sentence (5 Marks)

1. What is the objective of Pradhan Mantri Awaas Yojana?
2. Define migrant labour.
3. What is the purpose of Jal Jeevan Mission?
4. Name two sectors covered under non-farm livelihoods.
5. What does Atma Nirbhar Bharat focus on?

Question Paper 2 (university Affiliated Colleges)

Community Engagement Project (Discipline Specific Core Course)
Course Code: COL4CEP
Total Marks: 20
Duration: 1 Hour

Q.1 Attempt the following Multiple-Choice Questions (1/2 mark each): (10 Marks)

1. Which program focuses on the health and well-being of pregnant women and newborns?

   a) Ayushman Bharat
   b) Pradhan Mantri Matru Vandana Yojana
   c) Beti Bachao, Beti Padhao
   d) Skill India Mission

1. Which local institution provides funds for small rural businesses?

   a) Panchayat Samiti
   b) Self-Help Groups (SHGs)
   c) Municipal Corporation
   d) Zilla Parishad

3. The primary aim of Jal Jeevan Mission is to:

   a) Promote digital literacy
   b) Improve sanitation facilities
   c) Provide safe drinking water
   d) Increase employment

4. Gram Panchayat falls under which form of governance?

   a) Central government
   b) State government
   c) Local self-government
   d) Non-governmental organization

5. Which program is dedicated to enhancing rural connectivity by constructing roads?

   a) NRLM
   b) PMGSY (Pradhan Mantri Gram Sadak Yojana)
   c) Swachh Bharat Mission
   d) Atma Nirbhar Bharat

6. Atma Nirbhar Bharat promotes:

   a) Self-reliance and local production
   b) Tourism industry
   c) Import of luxury goods
   d) Sports development

7. Ayushman Bharat mainly benefits:

   a) School children
   b) Women in rural areas
   c) Individuals needing healthcare in low-income groups
   d) Farmers

8. The Scheme of Fund for Regeneration of Traditional Industries (SFURTI) primarily aims to:

   a) Boost the IT sector
   b) Develop traditional and artisan industries
   c) Support large manufacturing industries
   d) Fund educational initiatives

9. In India, which institution is primarily responsible for conducting village-level elections?

   a) Gram Panchayat
   b) Zilla Parishad
   c) Panchayat Samiti
   d) Municipal Corporation

10. Which program focuses on providing rural employment for at least 100 days?

    a) Ayushman Bharat
    b) Jal Jeevan Mission
    c) MGNREGA
    d) Sarva Shiksha Abhiyan

11. National Rural Livelihood Mission (NRLM) is implemented to:

    a) Provide healthcare in rural areas
    b) Strengthen SHGs to promote livelihoods
    c) Develop urban infrastructure
    d) Enhance literacy rates

12. The primary purpose of Pradhan Mantri Awaas Yojana is:

    a) Employment generation
    b) Affordable housing
    c) Women's empowerment
    d) Rural sanitation

13. SHGs primarily serve which group?

    a) Students
    b) Farmers
    c) Women in rural areas
    d) Senior citizens

14. The term "local economy" primarily refers to:

    a) International trade
    b) Urban commerce only
    c) Economic activities within a specific locality
    d) National economic policies

15. The Gram Panchayat reports directly to:

a) Central Government
b) Zilla Parishad
c) Municipal Corporation
d) Ministry of Education

16. Which program focuses on providing quality education to all children in India?

a) Swachh Bharat Mission
b) Sarva Shiksha Abhiyan
c) NRLM
d) Skill India Mission

17. Which organization typically facilitates the implementation of skill development in villages?

a) Municipal Corporations
b) Local SHGs
c) District Collector's office
d) Zilla Parishad

18. Migrant labourers primarily move to urban areas in search of:

a) Education
b) Financial loans
c) Employment
d) Medical facilities

19. The local economy in rural areas is usually dependent on:

a) Industries
b) Services
c) Agriculture
d) International trade

20. Which scheme aims to provide digital literacy to rural households?

a) NRLM

b) Digital India

c) Skill India

d) Swachh Bharat Mission

Q.2 Attempt the following:

A) Explain the terms/concepts (5 Marks)

1. Pradhan Mantri Awaas Yojana
2. Zilla Parishad
3. Atma Nirbhar Bharat
4. Migrant Labour
5. Panchayat Samiti

B) Answer the following in one sentence (5 Marks)

1. What is the aim of Pradhan Mantri Gram Sadak Yojana?
2. Define a Self-Help Group (SHG).
3. What does the Ayushman Bharat program focus on?
4. What is the role of local self-government?
5. State one objective of Sarva Shiksha Abhiyan.

Question Paper-3 (university Affiliated Colleges)

Community Engagement Project (Discipline Specific Core Course)
Course Code: COL4CEP
Total Marks: 20
Duration: 1 Hour

Q.1 Attempt the following Multiple-Choice Questions (1/2 mark each): (10 Marks)

1. The primary objective of Sarva Shiksha Abhiyan is:

   a) Employment generation
   b) Universal elementary education
   c) Rural sanitation
   d) Housing for all

1. The Mahatma Gandhi National Rural Employment Guarantee Act (MGNREGA) is designed to provide:

   a) Healthcare services
   b) Skill development
   c) Basic education
   d) Guaranteed employment

3. Which scheme is aimed at reducing infant mortality and maternal mortality rates?

   a) Beti Bachao, Beti Padhao
   b) MGNREGA
   c) Pradhan Mantri Matru Vandana Yojana
   d) Skill India Mission

4. National Rural Livelihood Mission (NRLM) focuses on:

   a) Women's economic empowerment
   b) Housing for all
   c) Digital education

d) Urban employment

5. Which scheme supports small artisans in setting up traditional industries?

   a) SFURTI
   b) Ayushman Bharat
   c) Jal Jeevan Mission
   d) Digital India

6. The Gram Panchayat functions under which level of governance?

   a) State
   b) District
   c) Local
   d) National

7. Atma Nirbhar Bharat aims to:

   a) Develop local employment only
   b) Increase self-sufficiency and reduce imports
   c) Boost urban development
   d) Promote foreign investments

8. Which body handles elementary education in rural India?

   a) Gram Panchayat
   b) Zilla Parishad
   c) Sarva Shiksha Abhiyan
   d) Municipal Corporation

9. Self-help Groups mainly provide:

   a) Health benefits
   b) Micro-finance and community support
   c) Urban infrastructure
   d) Rural sanitation

10. Which program focuses on skill development for various industries?

a) Digital India
b) Skill India
c) Ayushman Bharat
d) Swachh Bharat

11. The primary aim of the Beti Bachao, Beti Padhao scheme is:

a) Employment for women
b) Gender equality and education for girls
c) Rural development
d) Financial aid for families

12. The Skill India initiative helps individuals gain:

a) Foreign education
b) Vocational training
c) Employment in government services
d) Housing assistance

13. Which institution operates at the district level for rural governance?

a) Gram Sabha
b) Panchayat Samiti
c) Zilla Parishad
d) Municipal Corporation

14. Pradhan Mantri Awaas Yojana primarily focuses on:

a) Urban housing
b) Skill development
c) Rural sanitation
d) Affordable housing for low-income families

15. Local markets in rural areas primarily deal with:

a) International goods

b) Agricultural and artisanal products
c) Industrial machinery
d) Foreign imports

16. Gram Sabha meetings are held for:

a) Deciding national policies
b) Community decision-making at the village level
c) Supervising state administration
d) Regulating taxes

17. Which scheme focuses on healthcare and health insurance?

a) Sarva Shiksha Abhiyan
b) Ayushman Bharat
c) Swachh Bharat
d) Skill India

18. The primary goal of SFURTI is to:

a) Fund large corporations
b) Regenerate traditional industries
c) Build rural roads
d) Provide drinking water

19. Municipal Corporations primarily operate in:

a) Villages
b) Metropolitan and urban areas
c) Districts
d) Rural areas

20. Which of the following focuses on the empowerment of women and girls in rural areas?

a) Jal Jeevan Mission
b) Beti Bachao, Beti Padhao
c) Digital India

d) MGNREGA

Q.2 Attempt the following:

A) Explain the terms/concepts (5 Marks)

1. Pradhan Mantri Gram Sadak Yojana
2. Gram Sabha
3. Skill India Mission
4. Migrant Workers
5. Atma Nirbhar Bharat

B) Answer the following in one sentence (5 Marks)

1. What is the aim of the Beti Bachao, Beti Padhao scheme?
2. Define micro-finance.
3. State the purpose of SFURTI.
4. What is the role of Zilla Parishad?
5. Mention one goal of MGNREGA

Community Engagement Project Report

Student's Name:___________________________________
Roll Number:_____________________________________
Course Code: ____________________________________
Batch:____
Institution Name:_________________________________
Title of Report:_____________________________________
Topic of Study:___________________________________

Table of Contents

1. Acknowledgments

Express gratitude to individuals, community leaders, organizations, and faculty who assisted with your project.

2. Executive Summary

Summarize the objective, scope, key findings, and conclusions of your research in 200-300 words.

3. Introduction

- **Background:** Provide a brief background on the topic chosen.
- **Importance of Study:** Explain why this topic is relevant to community engagement and development.
- **Scope:** Describe the scope of the study, including community locations and populations targeted.

4. Objectives

State the main objectives of your research clearly, such as:

- Understanding local livelihood practices.
- Analyzing the effectiveness of national development programs.
- Assessing the role of local government institutions.

5. Research Methodology

Describe the research approach, methods, and tools used for data collection, such as interviews, surveys, or observations.

6. Schedule of Community Visits

Date DD/MM/YY	Location/Community Place Village name, SHG office, etc.	Objective of Visit e.g., Meet with local leaders	Activities/Tasks Undertaken Conducted interviews with community members	Notes/Observations Key observations noted
DD/MM/YY	Location details	Purpose of the visit	Research activities	Observations made

7. Observations

Provide detailed observations from each community visit. Describe:

- **Local Economic Activities:** Livelihood practices, market dynamics, etc.
- **Social Structure:** Role of SHGs, local institutions, etc.
- **Community Challenges and Opportunities:** Any barriers or promising trends observed.

8. Findings and Analysis

Summarize the findings from the research. Include:

- Key insights from community discussions.
- Analysis of how national development programs (e.g., MGNREGA, Skill India) are functioning in the community.
- Evaluation of local government effectiveness.

Use tables, charts, or graphs where possible to present quantitative data or trends.

9. Recommendations

Based on the findings, provide recommendations to address any issues observed or to enhance the community's development. For example:

- Suggested improvements in government program implementation.
- Potential community-led initiatives.
- Ideas for further student involvement.

10. Conclusion

Summarize the overall impact of your findings and reflect on how the experience has contributed to your understanding of community engagement.

11. References

List all resources, including government reports, academic references, and any other relevant sources consulted.

12. Appendix

Include supplementary materials such as:

- Interview questions.
- Survey forms.
- Photographs (if permitted by the community) to document field visits.

Notes for Submission:

- **Formatting:** Use Times New Roman, font size 12, 1.5 line spacing.
- **Word Limit:** 1,000-2,000 words.
- **Submission Deadline:** [Insert Deadline]
- **Submission Format:** Print/Soft copy as specified by your course instructor.

www.ingramcontent.com/pod-product-compliance
Lightning Source LLC
LaVergne TN
LVHW041128150826
845673LV00007B/2231

* 9 7 9 8 8 9 6 3 2 6 6 1 8 *